AN EASY GUIDE

PETER DOWLING

REGIONS OF NEW ZEALAND

New Zealand/Aotearoa is a medium-sized island country that has a wide range of landscapes, environments and people.

Regions recognise these differences and help organise society. People also define themselves by regions, districts or even neighbourhoods. The boundaries of local government define the regions of New Zealand.

The 16 regions on the map — and in this book — follow the outlines of New Zealand local government. Nelson and Tasman are officially different regions, but we will discuss them together.

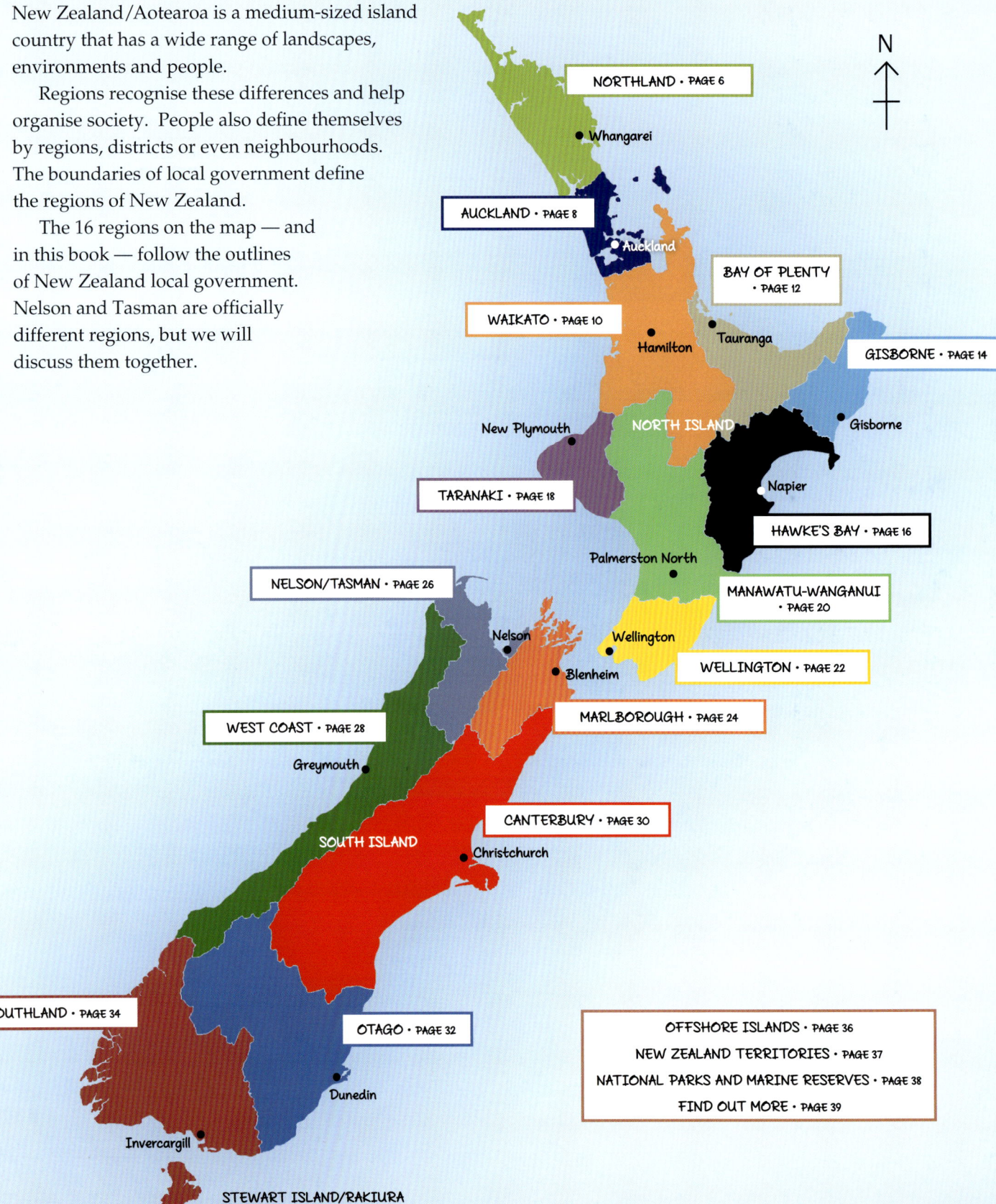

NORTHLAND · PAGE 6
AUCKLAND · PAGE 8
BAY OF PLENTY · PAGE 12
WAIKATO · PAGE 10
GISBORNE · PAGE 14
TARANAKI · PAGE 18
HAWKE'S BAY · PAGE 16
MANAWATU-WANGANUI · PAGE 20
NELSON/TASMAN · PAGE 26
WELLINGTON · PAGE 22
WEST COAST · PAGE 28
MARLBOROUGH · PAGE 24
CANTERBURY · PAGE 30
SOUTHLAND · PAGE 34
OTAGO · PAGE 32

OFFSHORE ISLANDS · PAGE 36
NEW ZEALAND TERRITORIES · PAGE 37
NATIONAL PARKS AND MARINE RESERVES · PAGE 38
FIND OUT MORE · PAGE 39

NGĀ ROHE MĀORI — MĀORI REGIONS

After arriving in Aotearoa from Tahiti or Rarotonga around 800 years ago, Māori discovered and named the different regions. Naming of coasts, mountains, rivers and lakes helped to define areas and people's connections to them.

Māori lived in regions they defined as rohe or takiwā. Their communities held responsibilities to the land and environment, captured by the modern term mana whenua — meaning authority of people over land.

The community groups were usually small hapū (collectives) of extended whānau (families) who were related. Today Māori still organise themselves as whānau and hapū, but also as larger collectives of hapū called iwi (tribe).

All levels of community — whānau, hapū and iwi, as well as collectives of iwi — exercise rights and custodial duties over lands or regions.

At the highest level, Aotearoa can be divided into the nine regions shown on this map. These are reflected in some electorate and land court boundaries. The map also indicates some of the largest iwi groups. Discussion between iwi concerning boundaries of rohe continues today.

YESTERDAY AND TODAY

Local government

New Zealand is divided into regions and districts for the purposes of local government. Local government is made up of the politicians and public servants who administer these areas.

Central government, based in Wellington, is responsible for national issues. It set the boundaries and roles for the current regions in the late 1980s and early 1990s. Within each region are districts, which have their own administrations and services.

Today there are 11 regional councils and 67 territorial authorities. The authorities consist of 53 district councils, 12 city councils, Auckland Council and the Chatham Islands Council.

> People often identify more with their district than with the wider region — especially offshore in places such as Stewart Island, the Chathams or 'the Barrier' (Great Barrier Island)

The Canterbury Provincial Council Buildings in Christchurch, home of Canterbury's provincial government until 1876. Following damage in the 2010 and 2011 Canterbury earthquakes, the buildings are being reconstructed.

The Provinces

Wellington was not always the centre of government. Nor has a central government always ruled New Zealand.

Māori leaders and the British Crown signed the Treaty of Waitangi in various regions throughout 1840. Following this, a governor administered New Zealand. It was difficult for the governor to be everywhere at once, so in 1846 the country was divided into two provinces: New Ulster (the North Island) and New Munster (the South Island and Stewart Island/Rakiura).

In 1852 the New Zealand Constitution Act created provinces that developed into what is shown on the map. Provinces had wider powers than regional governments do today, and some covered very large areas.

In 1876 the provinces were abolished as the colony expanded. Improving communications and transport made it easier to administer the colony from the capital. But provinces continued to be important divisions of local government until the 1990s, as seen on the lower map.

Period	Capital city	Largest city
1840	Kororāreka (Russell)	———
1841	Auckland	Wellington
1865	Wellington	Dunedin
1965	Wellington	Auckland
2017	Wellington	Auckland

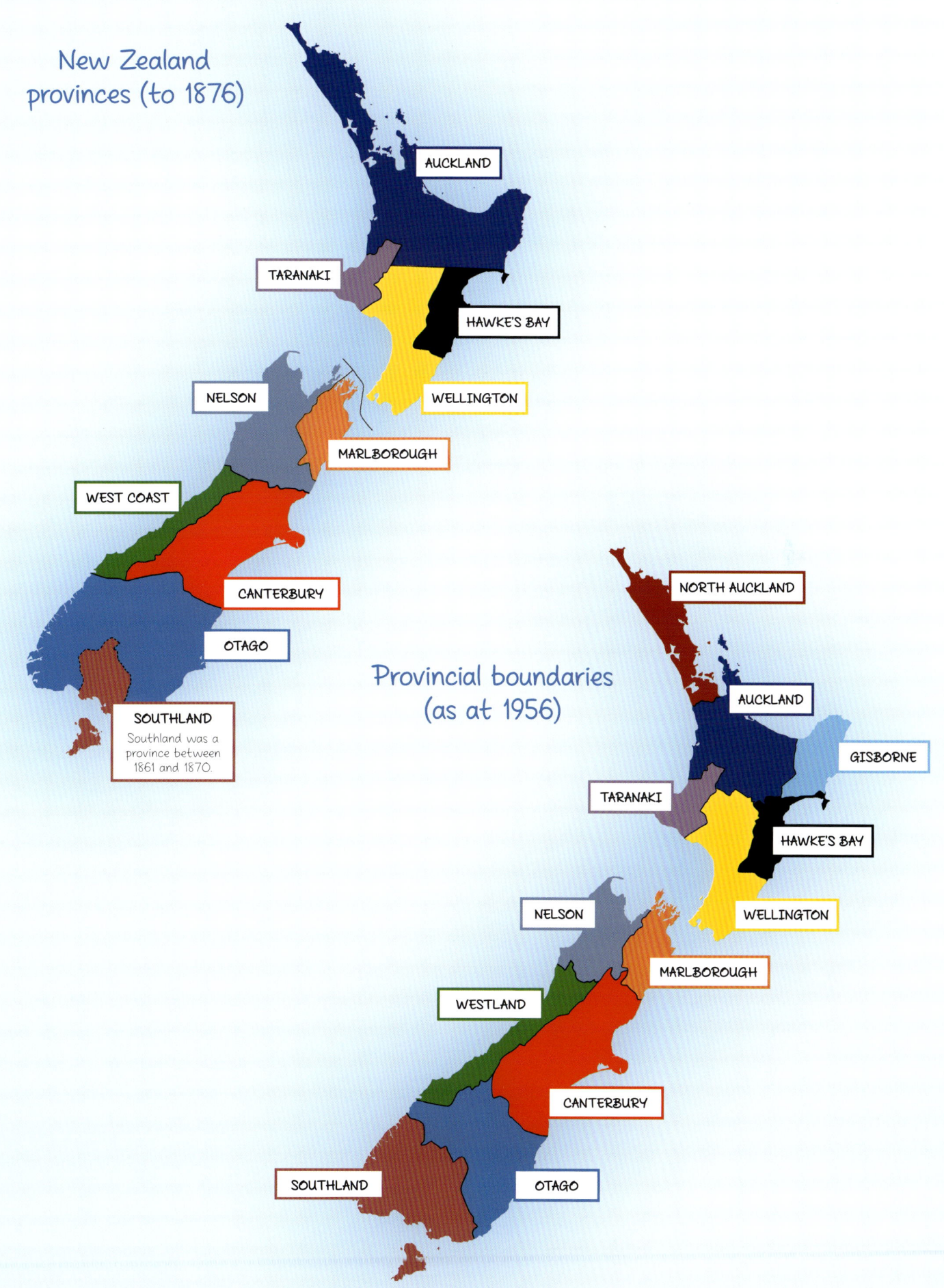

NORTHLAND
TE TAI TOKERAU

Tane Mahuta, the giant kauri tree in Northland's Waipoua Forest.

New Zealand's northernmost region extends 250 kilometres from North Cape to the Kaipara Harbour. It is home to just over 170,000 people.

Northland (Te Tai Tokerau in Māori) has a large Māori population, including the largest iwi (tribe), Ngāpuhi. Māori believe that Cape Reinga, in the Far North, is where spirits of the dead leave for the homeland of Hawaiki.

Europeans settled in Northland from the 1810s. Their whaling, logging, gum digging and farming changed the environment. History, beaches, diving and fishing attract many tourists to the Bay of Islands, the Waipoua Forest and Ninety Mile Beach.

In the past, job creation in Northland has been difficult. However, in recent years development has increased. Whangārei has grown as a port and industrial centre, and nearby Marsden Point is New Zealand's main oil refinery.

It's a fact!

Area 12,498 square kilometres*
Population 171,400*
Main industries Beef farming, boat building, forestry, tourism
Did you know? Northland is the warmest region in New Zealand.

The carved meeting house in the Waitangi Treaty Grounds.

Cape Reinga, at the extreme north of the North Island.

BAY OF ISLANDS

The Bay of Islands is one of the jewels of Northland. Russell (Kororāreka) was the first Pākehā (New Zealand European) town and the main point of contact with Māori through the 1830s. The area still shows signs of early trade and conflict between Māori and Pākehā. Today Kerikeri and Paihia are among the fastest-growing towns in the country, enjoying a sunny climate and a busy tourist trade.

The beautiful Bay of Islands.

* Land area information is from the Department of Internal Affairs, Local Councils website, http://www.localcouncils.govt.nz/lgip.nsf/wpg_URL/Profiles-Councils-by-Region, accessed 8 June 2017. Population figures are from Statistics New Zealand sub-national population estimates at 30 June 2016, accessed 8 June 2017.

AUCKLAND TĀMAKI-MAKAURAU

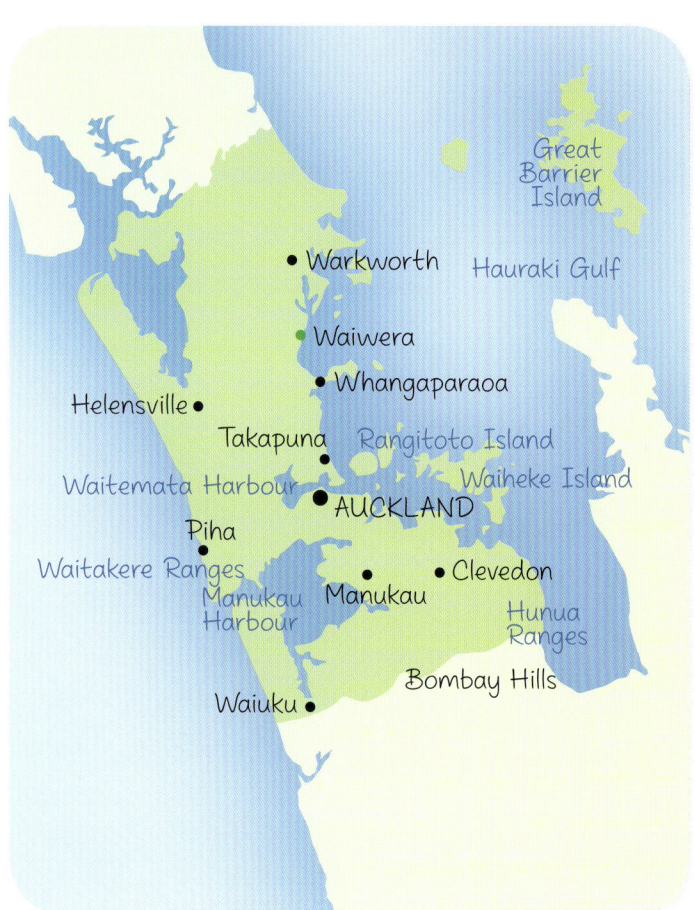

Auckland is New Zealand's largest region by population and among its smallest by land area. It is centred on the Auckland isthmus, a volcanic area that is much desired by for its rich soils and sea resources — hence the name Tāmaki-makaurau (Tamaki desired by 100 lovers).

Auckland City is home to about one-third of New Zealand's residents, and is growing fast due to immigration. It ranks among the most liveable cities in the world. Auckland's port and airport are the main entry and exit points for New Zealand, and many of the country's largest companies are based here.

This region extends out into the Hauraki Gulf to Waiheke Island and across to Great Barrier Island, offering beaches, fishing and sailing spots. Balancing its natural attractions with a growing population is the region's main challenge, as suburbs take over farmlands and traffic worsens.

Waiheke Island is one of the jewels of the Hauraki Gulf.

Auckland, with sports stadium Eden Park in the foreground.

It's a fact!

Area 4938 square kilometres
Population 1,614,400
Main industries Business services, construction, health, hospitality and tourism, manufacturing
Did you know? Auckland is the largest city in Polynesia, and has almost 200,000 residents of Pacific Island descent.

What's an isthmus? An isthmus is a strip of land that lies between two larger pieces of land.

Multicultural Auckland on stage at the annual ASB Polyfest festival.

THE WILD WEST

Karekare beach.

Auckland's West Coast is wild! From the forested Waitakere Ranges, cliffs and valleys plunge to black-sand beaches. Waves crashing from the Tasman Sea draw surfers and swimmers to Karekare, Piha, Te Henga (Bethells) and Muriwai, but care is needed. Television shows such as *Piha Rescue* show how dangerous the seas can be.

WAIKATO

The Huka Falls, near the source of the Waikato River.

Rich green pastures make Waikato the heart of dairy farming. The region is home to over 30% of dairy herds in New Zealand. Some of the nation's most expensive farmland is found between the Waikato River and the Hauraki Plains. The river is home to extensive hydro-electric generation schemes and New Zealand's only large coal-fired power station (at Huntly).

This region also takes in the ranges and beaches of the Coromandel Peninsula, the rugged western harbours of Raglan and Kawhia, and the forest and lakelands of Taupo. Hamilton is the country's fourth-biggest city, and is home to manufacturing industries and the University of Waikato.

The largest Māori university, Te Wānanga o Aotearoa, is based in Te Awamutu, while Ngaruawahia is the home of the Māori king, the leader of the Waikato-Tainui people. Since featuring in the *Lord of the Rings* and *Hobbit* movies, the Hobbiton Movie Set near Matamata has become a major tourist attraction.

It's a fact!

Area 23,902 square kilometres
Population 449,200
Main industries Agricultural science, coal mining, dairy farming, forestry, horse breeding
Did you know? The Waikato River is the longest river in New Zealand and Lake Taupo is the largest lake.

The Hobbiton Movie Set, near Matamata.

Holidaymakers at Hot Water Beach, on the Coromandel Peninsula.

WAITOMO

Limestone rock has left this district southwest of Hamilton marked with caves and interesting rock formations. The famous Waitomo Caves attract many visitors with their underground formations and glow-worms. The Waitomo area also has different weather patterns from other parts of Waikato, and is mentioned separately in weather reports.

Inside the Waitomo Caves.

BAY OF PLENTY
TE MOANA-A-TOI

Captain Cook named this region because he was able to get food there in 1769. The Bay of Plenty continues to be a major producer of food — the kiwifruit industry is based around Te Puke.

Tauranga has grown to be the fifth-largest city in the country, and its port is now the second busiest after Auckland. The regional council, however, is based in Whakatane.

Plentiful sunshine draws visitors to the coastline as well, from Waihi Beach in the west along to Mount Maunganui, Ohope and Whakatane. The climate also makes this a popular area for older people to retire.

The Port of Tauranga with the city behind.

Whakaari/White Island.

It's a fact!

Area 12,071 square kilometres
Population 293,500
Main industries Dairy and beef farming, forestry, fruit growing, tourism
Did you know? Whakaari/White Island is New Zealand's most active volcano.

Lake Tarawera, close to Rotorua.

ROTORUA

Descendants of the Arawa canoe have a proud culture and political voice in Rotorua, a city of 65,000 people. Māori culture and the volcanic landscape make this one of New Zealand's major tourist centres. Geysers, hot pools and boiling mud feature in this spectacular landscape. Rotorua mud is said to be very good for the skin!

Woodcarving traditions live on in Rotorua.

GISBORNE
TE TAI RĀWHITI

In terms of population and area Gisborne is among the smallest regions, and also the farthest from the main centres. What it lacks in size, it makes up for in culture, lifestyle and sunshine.

East Cape marks the easternmost point of the North Island. South from here along Highway 35 are quiet settlements and an attractive coastline. The East Coast area, known as Te Tai Rāwhiti in Māori, is the heartland of Ngāti Porou, the second-largest iwi in the country. About half the people living here are Māori.

The port city of Gisborne (Tūranganui-a-Kiwa) has most of the region's population. This is the administrative and service centre, a relaxed city surrounded by beaches, farmlands and vineyards.

The National Arboretum at Eastwoodhill.

It's a fact!

Area 8386 square kilometres
Population 47,800
Main industries Farming, fisheries, forestry, fruit growing
Did you know? The National Arboretum (tree collection) is at Eastwoodhill, 35 kilometres outside Gisborne.

Sponge Bay Island, a popular surfing spot near Gisborne.

Gisborne city.

LANDING PLACES

Gisborne and the East Coast were the first lands reached by many voyagers to Aotearoa New Zealand. Waka (canoes) including the Takitimu and Horouta voyaged here from Polynesia. Whangara, north of Gisborne, was the arrival point of the ancestor Paikea, who is said to have travelled on the back of a whale. And it was at the Tūranganui River in Gisborne that Captain James Cook and his crew first set foot on New Zealand soil, on 8 October 1769.

Carving of Paikea atop the Whitireia meeting house, Whangara.

HAWKE'S BAY HERETAUNGA

Art Deco style in Napier.

A sunny and fertile region, Hawke's Bay is famous for food and wine, hot summers and crisp winters, rolling hills and coastal surf. The climate is dry and sunny, suitable for grape growing and sheep farming.

Most of its people live in the central area between Napier, Hastings and Havelock North. The north and south of the region are home to farming communities.

One of the most damaging earthquakes in New Zealand's history hit here in 1931. Napier and Hastings were rebuilt in Art Deco style, which today forms one of the mainstays of local tourism and is celebrated with an Art Deco weekend in Napier. The cities enjoy friendly competition over which has the best architecture — but put aside rivalry when it comes to supporting the local Magpies rugby team.

Gannets at Cape Kidnappers.

It's a fact!

Area 14,137 square kilometres
Population 161,500
Main industries Fruit growing, sheep and beef farming, tourism, winemaking
Did you know? The world's largest mainland gannet colony is at Cape Kidnappers, east of Hastings.

PANIA OF THE REEF

A small statue on the Napier waterfront, unveiled in 1954, honours the memory of the Māori heroine, Pania. She was a woman of the sea who fell in love with a young chief, lived with him and had a child, but would return to the sea every morning. When her husband tried to keep her on land, Pania was broken-hearted. She turned into a rock that can still be seen in the reef out from Napier.

The statue of Pania on the Napier seafront.

Wairoa's famous lighthouse.

✸ New Zealand's longest place name describes a hill near Porangahau: Taumatawhakatangihangakoauauotamateaturipukakakapikimaungahoronukupokaiwhenuakitanatahu (count the letters!).

TARANAKI

Dawson Falls, Egmont National Park.

Taranaki is defined by the mountain that sits at its heart: Mount Egmont or Taranaki. Taranaki was a province from the 1850s (it was first called New Plymouth province). There was bitter conflict here during the New Zealand Wars, and the village of Parihaka was the site of a peaceful campaign by Māori to resist land sales.

Since those days, the region has shown steady development. New Plymouth is the centre of national oil and gas production, and the rich lands support valuable dairy farming. Average incomes per person are higher in Taranaki than in any other region.

Taranaki also has a vibrant cultural scene, exemplified by New Plymouth's artistic waterfront and annual music festivals such as WOMAD.

TARANAKI'S GREAT MOUNTAIN

The mountain is officially called 'Mount Egmont or Mount Taranaki' to reflect the two names it bears. Captain Cook gave the English name in January 1770 to honour the Earl of Egmont. The Māori name means 'shining peak', and is the most commonly used name today. Legend says that the 2518-metre volcano had to move here after losing to Mount Tongariro in a battle for the love of the mountain Pihanga. A national park surrounds the mountain, marking a neat circle on the map.

New Plymouth.

It's a fact!

Area 7254 square kilometres
Population 116,700
Main industries Dairy farming, petrochemicals
Did you know? All New Zealand's oil and natural gas production is drawn from the sea to the west of Taranaki.

Taranaki's iconic mountain.

Oil drilling at the Sidewinder site, near Inglewood.

MANAWATU-WANGANUI
MANAWATŪ ME WHANGANUI

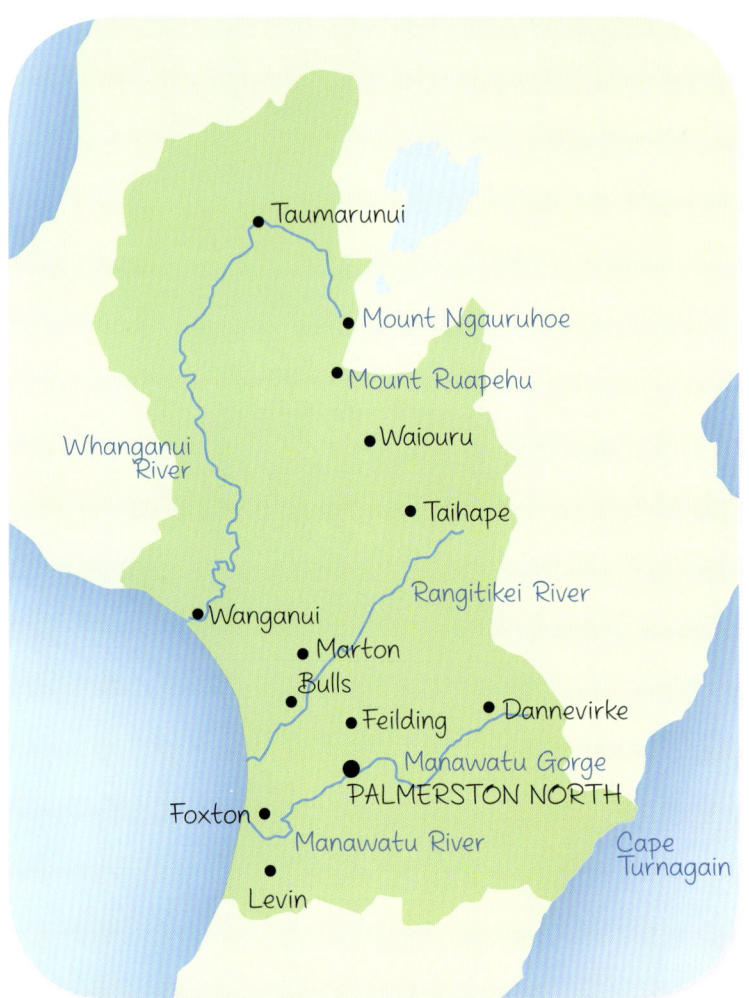

Manawatu and Wanganui are two historic regions now joined as one. They are defined by mighty rivers: the Manawatu, the Rangitikei and the Whanganui. The rivers descend from the Ruahine and Tararua ranges and the volcanic plateau, feeding rich plains for farming.

Massey University is an important centre of agricultural science in the region's largest city, Palmerston North. Towns like Bulls and Levin draw their life from the fertile plains.

The northern Ruapehu district takes in Tongariro National Park, with its volcanos and ski fields. Whanganui National Park encircles the upper reaches of the Whanganui River, a spiritual land that inspired the poet James K. Baxter among others.

Mount Ruapehu, on the volcanic plateau.

20

It's a fact!

Area 22,220 square kilometres
Population 236,900
Main industries Agricultural science, defence, education, sheep and beef farming
Did you know? Residents of Whangamomona declared themselves a republic in protest at being placed in the Manawatu-Wanganui region in 1989.

Manawatu's rich farmlands.

Palmerston North.

WHANGANUI OR WANGANUI

Māori in the Whanganui rohe don't pronounce the 'h'. That's largely why European settlers recorded the location called Whanganui — meaning big bay — as Wanganui. In the early 2000s, there was fierce debate locally about a move to rename the town. The New Zealand Geographic Board agreed to allow both spellings of the name for the city; the river is officially spelled Whanganui.

The Whanganui River.

WELLINGTON
TE UPOKO O TE IKA

Night sky at Castlepoint.

Wellington region is made up of two distinct sub-regions: Wellington and the Kapiti Coast to the west, and Wairarapa to the east. These two sub-regions are divided by the steep hills of the Rimutaka and Tararua ranges.

Wellington was founded in 1840 by the New Zealand Company as an 'instant city', and became national capital in 1865. It is famous for its striking harbour, its wind and, in recent years, a world-class film industry.

From here, State Highway 1 threads north past the beaches and coves of the Kapiti Coast. The Wairarapa Coast, by contrast, is isolated and wild. The countryside around Masterton and Martinborough is gentler, and is developing as a lifestyle and winemaking destination.

Along the Kapiti Coast.

The Wellington Cable Car, Kelburn.

It's a fact!

Area 8049 square kilometres
Population 504,800
Main industries Agriculture, education, film, government, winemaking
Did you know? Wellington people enjoy the highest incomes per person of any New Zealand city.

Inside the Weta Workshop film studio.

PARLIAMENT

Parliament stands at the heart of the so-called government precinct in central Wellington — a cluster of key government departments and the law courts. Parliament itself comprises several major buildings including the Executive Wing, nicknamed The Beehive because of its distinctive shape. The Parliamentary Library is the oldest of the buildings.

The Beehive.

MARLBOROUGH
TE TAU IHU O TE WAKA-A-MĀUI*

A region of dry soils, plentiful sun and low rainfall, Marlborough originally developed an economy based on sheep farming.

The city of Blenheim grew as a service centre for farming. Transport connections were also important, with Picton being the southern end of the ferry service across Cook Strait from Wellington.

In recent decades, the wine industry has boomed in this region. Soils and climate around the city of Blenheim and in the Wairau Valley have proved ideal for making wine, most famously Sauvignon Blanc. Marlborough now produces about three-quarters of New Zealand's wine.

Tourism has followed the wine industry. That has encouraged new ventures such as the Omaka Air Heritage Centre, which has a large collection of historic aircraft and artefacts. Forestry and marine farming are also important to Marlborough.

Marlborough is renowned for grapes and wine.

*Te Tau Ihu o te Waka-a-Māui refers to all the northern part of the South Island.

The Waihopai Valley.

It's a fact!

Area 10,458 square kilometres
Population 45,500
Main industries Aquaculture, sheep and beef farming, tourism, winemaking
Did you know? Marlborough has New Zealand's largest farm — the 180,787-hectare Molesworth Station.

THE MARLBOROUGH SOUNDS

'The Sounds', as locals know them, are actually sunken valleys. Queen Charlotte and Pelorus sounds, the two main arms, lead into beautiful harbours with picturesque beaches. Early Māori navigators, like Captain Cook after them, appreciated the sheltered harbours; many areas can still be reached only by boat.

Queen Charlotte Sound/Tōtaranui.

Picton, where the Cook Strait ferry reaches the South Island.

NELSON AND TASMAN
TE TAU IHU O TE WAKA-A-MĀUI*

The city of Nelson, and the mostly rural region of Tasman, occupy the northwestern corner of the South Island. Richmond is the seat of the Tasman District Council.

Nelson was founded in 1842 and is one of New Zealand's most historic cities. One of the sunniest parts of New Zealand, this region is important for crop and fruit growing. Port Nelson is a major base for commercial fishing. The area is well known for arts and crafts, such as pottery.

To the northwest, Golden Bay/Te Taitapu is a relatively unpopulated area with golden-sand beaches. People come here for the relaxed lifestyle, with Germans among the more recent settlers.

Nature abounds here. Three national parks are found within Tasman/Nelson's borders (it shares Kahurangi National Park with the West Coast). Prominent nature reserves such as Farewell Spit add to its natural charms.

Kayaking around Abel Tasman National Park.

*Te Tau Ihu o te Waka-a-Māui refers to all the northern part of the South Island.

NELSON

A view over Nelson city.

It's a fact!

Area Nelson 424 square kilometres, Tasman 9616 square kilometres
Population 100,800 (combined)
Main industries Fisheries, forestry, fruit growing, tourism
Did you know? The geographical centre of New Zealand is located in Nelson city.

Why is Nelson separate from Tasman? Nelson City Council is the unitary authority for the city area, while Tasman District Council is the authority for the rural area. Nelson is actually a 'unitary authority', combining a city and regional government, while Tasman is a region in itself. Both have similar populations, and join with Marlborough to play as the Tasman Makos rugby team.

The centre of New Zealand.

Christ Church Cathedral, Nelson.

Farewell Spit.

WEST COAST
TE TAI POUTINI

Te Tai Poutini is the Māori name for the West Coast. Poutini is a guardian of pounamu (greenstone), and reflects the mineral wealth has long been a mainstay of life in this coastal region.

Māori traversed the Southern Alps to search for pounamu (greenstone) here. Europeans flocked to 'the Coast' to mine for gold in the nineteenth century. Coal mining is one of the last main mineral activities here, but is declining, however, hit by tragedies like the Pike River Mine disaster of November 2010.

The beautiful landscape in this thin stretch of land between the Tasman Sea and the Alps makes it a significant tourist destination. With less than 35,000 inhabitants it is the smallest region by population — and along with Fiordland, the wettest part of the country.

It's a fact!

Area 23,244 square kilometres
Population 32,500
Main industries Dairy farming, mining, tourism
Did you know? In August 1888 the town of Reefton became the first in the Southern Hemisphere to have electric street lighting.

Punakaiki's famous Pancake Rocks.

Panning for gold near Greymouth.

THE GLACIERS

Descending from the western side of the Southern Alps, Fox and Franz Josef glaciers extend close to the sea. The ease of accessing these rivers of ice draws visitors from around the world. Climate change is causing the glaciers to retreat inland, however. This has already lengthened the walk that visitors must make to reach them, and may change the landscape greatly in years to come.

Hokitika's Memorial Clock Tower.

Franz Josef Glacier/Kā Roimata o Hinehukatere.

CANTERBURY WAITAHA

The Canterbury Plains.

Canterbury is New Zealand's largest region by area. It extends from the Clarence River in the north to the Waitaki River in the south, from the Southern Alps in the west across the Canterbury Plains to Banks Peninsula in the east.

Christchurch is the social and economic centre of Canterbury. 'The Garden City' is rebuilding following the earthquakes of the early 2010s. Secondary centres including Rangiora and Rolleston have developed as people have relocated after the quakes.

Dairy, crop and fruit farming dominate activity on the Plains, the largest flat area in the country. Canterbury also is home to the highest mountain, Aoraki/Mount Cook (3724 metres). The Southern Alps and mighty rivers like the Waimakariri, Rakaia and Rangitata offer many outdoor experiences, one reason the region was the birthplace of brands such as Macpac and Kathmandu.

Little Regent Street, Christchurch.

> ## It's a fact!
>
> **Area** 44,508 square kilometres
> **Population** 599,900
> **Main industries** Business services, farming, manufacturing, technology, tourism
> **Did you know?** Banks Peninsula was settled by the French in the 1840s and still has a lot of French names in use.

Church of the Good Shepherd, Tekapo.

Looking towards Aoraki/Mount Cook.

KAIKOURA

Kaikoura was part of Nelson province until 1876, and for many years afterwards part of Marlborough (it is closer to Blenheim than it is to Christchurch). This picturesque town was badly damaged by a 7.8-magnitude shock on 14 November 2016. Kaikoura is counting on recovery thanks to its natural advantages — close to sea and mountains, a base for whale-watching, and sited on the main rail and road links north from Christchurch.

Seals near Kaikoura.

OTAGO
ŌTĀKOU

Dunedin was the leading city in New Zealand around the 1860s and 1870s. Its fine architecture and institutions testify to the riches created by gold and wool booms. Today, it is the University of Otago (the oldest in the country) that leads the city's economic activity.

Central Otago — 'Central' to its inhabitants — has boomed in recent years with increasing tourism. Queenstown and Wanaka have become expensive places to live as people move here for scenery and the outdoors. Where goldmining and farming once created fortunes, now it is adventure sports, tourism and winemaking that keep Central busy.

Central is dominated by the Clutha River, which is the country's largest waterway by volume, and powers important hydroelectric dams. It reaches the coast beyond Balclutha, its waters mixing with flows from the Southern Ocean.

Wanaka in winter.

It's a fact!

Area 31,209 square kilometres
Population 219,200
Main industries Education, farming, forestry, tourism, winemaking
Did you know? Larnach Castle on the Otago Peninsula is the only full-scale castle in New Zealand.

Baldwin Street, Dunedin — one of the world's steepest residential streets.

University of Otago, Dunedin.

MOERAKI BOULDERS/ KAIHINAKI

About 40 kilometres south of Oamaru, these round boulders were formed by lime salts over millions of years. Some are as much as four metres wide. Māori legend tells that these are the preserved food baskets (kaihinaki) washed ashore from the canoe Araiteuru.

The Moeraki Boulders/Kaihinaki.

Penguin on the Otago Peninsula.

SOUTHLAND MURIHIKU

Kea, Fiordland.

Invercargill.

Southland is a region of contrasts. At its western edge is Fiordland National Park, the country's largest — with popular locations like Milford Sound, as well as valleys where humans have hardly stepped foot.

The plains fed by rivers such as the Mataura yield rich farmlands. Dairy and sheep farming are serviced by prosperous towns such as Winton and Gore (the home of Kiwi country music). Invercargill, the main centre, is a flat city of wide roads. Nearby Bluff is home to a significant aluminium smelter, and produces the famous Bluff oysters. Across the rough seas of Foveaux Strait lies Stewart Island/Rakiura and many smaller islands.

Southland is the coldest part of the country, being closest to Antarctica, but its people are known for their warmth.

Farming in Southland.

It's a fact!

Area 31,195 square kilometres
Population 98,000
Main industries Aluminium manufacturing, dairy and sheep farming, forestry, tourism
Did you know? Southland people have a unique accent, rolling the letter 'r'.

Milford Sound/Piopiotahi.

STEWART ISLAND/RAKIURA

The third largest island in New Zealand at 1680 square kilometres, Stewart Island/Rakiura is home to fewer than 400 people. With so few humans around, nature abounds: Rakiura National Park covers most of the island, and is home to thousands of kiwi. Boat and plane services link the island to Bluff and Invercargill.

Tranquil Stewart Island.

OFFSHORE ISLANDS

Chatham Islands — Rekohu

Although it is not a local government region, the Chatham Islands is a special case in New Zealand.

This group of 11 islands has its own council, which was set up under the Chatham Islands Council Act 1995. The archipelago (group of islands) also has its own time zone, 45 minutes ahead of mainland New Zealand.

The first inhabitants were the Moriori, who called the island Rekohu. In 1835 Ngāti Mutunga and Ngāti Tama moved to the island, which they called Wharekauri, killing many Moriori in the process. Today about 600 people reside here, living mostly from farming, fisheries and tourism.

Chatham Island (the largest island) is about 650 kilometres from the nearest point on the North Island. New Zealand's most easterly point is out here — the Forty Fours/Motuhara Islands.

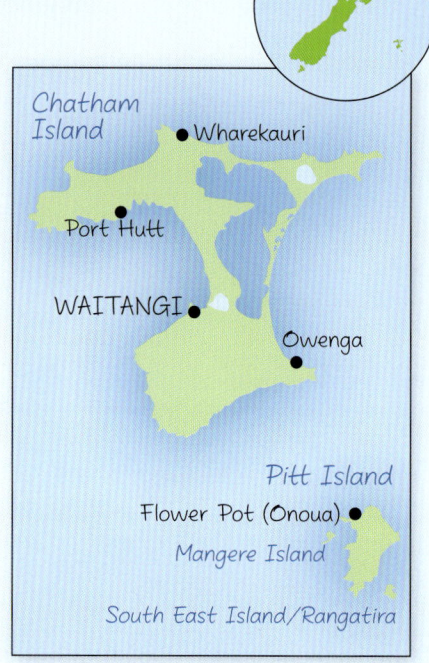

Kermadec Islands

The northernmost outpost of New Zealand, instead, is Raoul Island in the volcanic Kermadec Islands. These small islands are a nature reserve and marine reserve, with unique bird and sea life. Only a few scientists live here for any length of time.

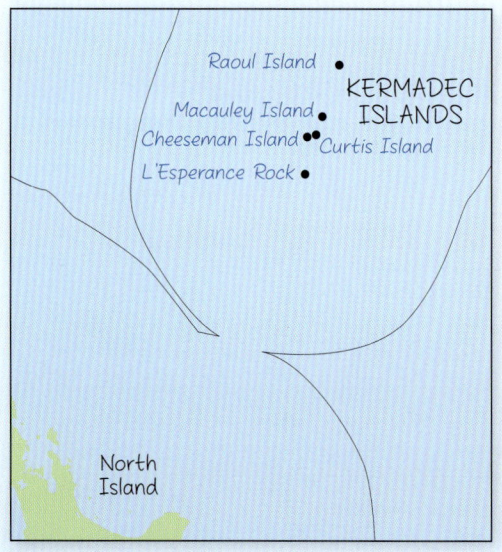

Subantarctic islands

The Auckland Islands are the largest group of these scattered islands, far to the south of Stewart Island. Campbell Island/Motu Ihupuku is the furthest south, lying about 700 kilometres from Invercargill. The other groups are the Antipodes Islands, the Bounty Islands, and the Snares Islands/Tini Heke.

Today the islands are nature reserves. Polynesian and European settlers came here in the past, but the terrible climate discouraged long stays — windy, wet and cold most of the time.

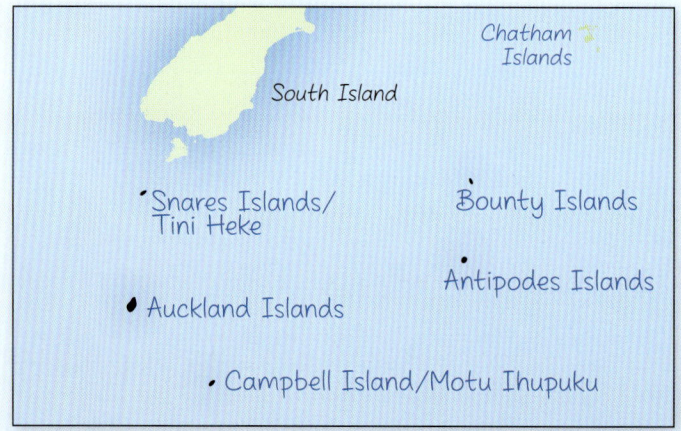

NEW ZEALAND TERRITORIES

Tokelau

The atolls (coral islands) of Atafu, Fakaofo and Nukunonu make up Tokelau. This territory of just 10 square kilometres lies 500 kilometres north of Samoa. New Zealand has administered Tokelau since 1925. The atolls are home to about 1300 people; over 7000 Tokelauans live in New Zealand.

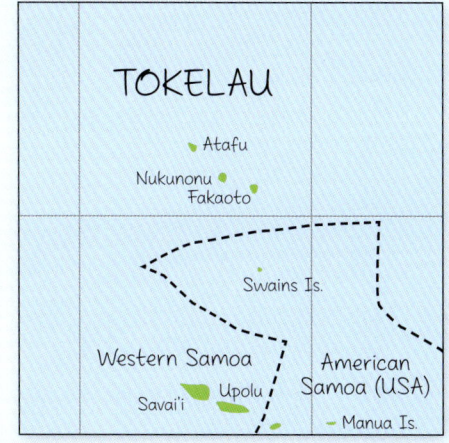

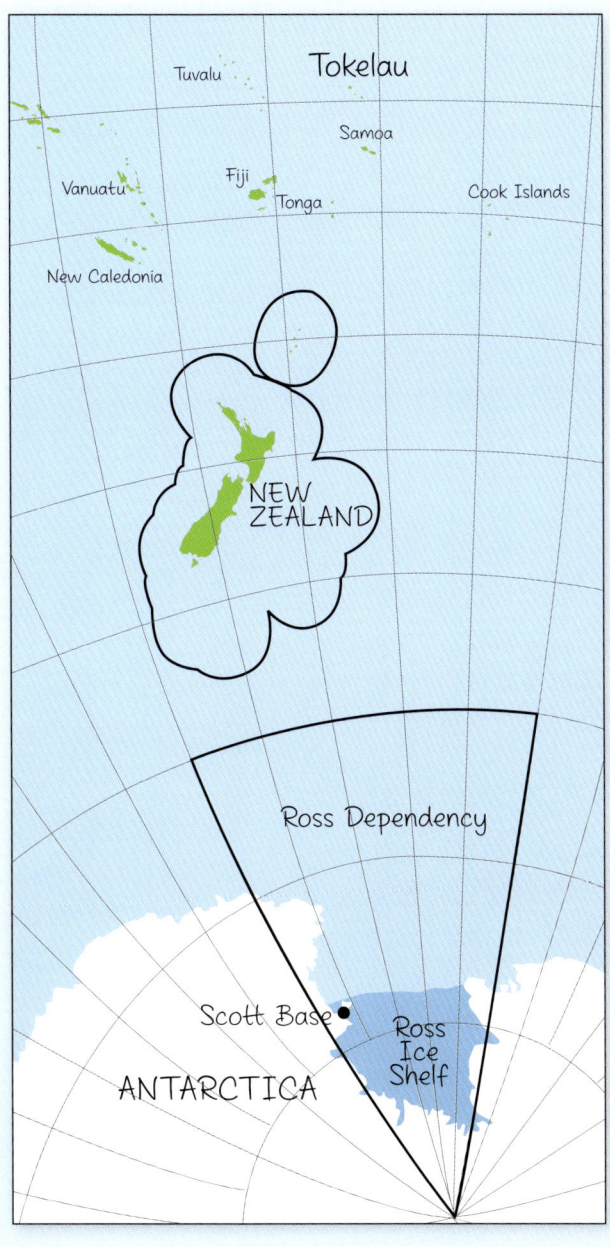

Antarctica: the Ross Dependency

The territory that New Zealand administers in Antarctica is immense — 450,000 square kilometres. The Ross Dependency, as the territory is known, is mostly sea, and includes the Ross Ice Shelf (which is about the same size as France).

The Ross Dependency has three bases where scientists and other staff live year round: New Zealand's Scott Base (founded in 1957), the American base of McMurdo Station, and Italy's Mario Zucchelli Station. Scott Base is some 3500 kilometres south of Dunedin.

The Ross Ice Shelf.

NATIONAL PARKS AND MARINE RESERVES

The Department of Conservation (DOC) administers New Zealand's 13 national parks — lands of supreme natural importance and scenic beauty. Since 2014, Te Urewera is no longer a national park.

DOC also oversees 44 marine reserves — protected areas of the coast and sea. Anyone can visit and enjoy these reserves, but you are not allowed to fish or disturb marine life there.

National Parks

Tongariro is the oldest national park; Rakiura is the newest.

Fiordland National Park is the largest, at 12,519 square kilometres.

National Parks labelled on map:
- Tongariro
- Egmont
- Whanganui
- Abel Tasman
- Kahurangi
- Paparoa
- Nelson Lakes
- Westland Tai Poutini
- Arthur's Pass
- Aoraki/Mount Cook
- Mount Aspiring
- Fiordland
- Rakiura

Marine Reserves

North Island:
- Poor Knights Islands
- Cape Rodney–Okakari Point (Goat Island)
- Tāwharanui
- Long Bay–Okura
- Te Matuku
- Whanganui a Hei (Cathedral Cove)
- Tuhua/Mayor Island
- Te Paepae o Aotea (Volkner Rocks)
- Whangarei Harbour
- Motu Manawa–Pollen Island
- Parininihi
- Tapuae

South Island:
- Horoirangi
- Tonga Island
- Westhaven (Te Tai Tapu)
- Kahurangi
- Kapiti
- Te Tapuwae o Rongokako
- Te Angiangi
- Taputeranga
- Punakaiki
- Long Island–Kokomohua
- Waiau Glacier Coast
- Hikurangi
- Tauparikākā
- Pōhatu (Flea Bay)
- Hautai
- Akaroa
- Fiordland (10 reserves)

Stewart Island/Rakiura:
- Ulva Island–Te Wharawhara

Offshore island reserves
- Kermadec Islands
- Bounty Islands/Moutere Hauriri
- Antipodes Islands/Moutere Mahue
- Campbell Islands/Moutere Ihupuku
- Auckland Islands/Motu Maha

FIND OUT MORE

Bibliography

BOOKS

Dowling, Peter and Forer, Pip (eds), *Reed New Zealand Atlas*, Reed Books, Auckland, 2004.

Kelly, Jan and Marshall, Brian, *Atlas of New Zealand Boundaries*, Auckland University Press, Auckland, 1996.

McKinnon, Malcolm (ed.), *New Zealand Historical Atlas*, David Bateman Ltd, Auckland, 1997.

Reed, A.W. & Dowling, Peter, *Place Names of New Zealand*, Penguin Books, Auckland, 2010.

Statistics New Zealand, *New Zealand in Profile 2015*, Statistics New Zealand, Wellington, 2015.

Wards, Ian (ed.), *New Zealand Atlas*, Government Printer, Wellington, 1976.

Wright, Matthew, *Reed Illustrated History of New Zealand*, Reed Books, Auckland, 2004.

WEBSITES

Check out these sites for more information.
Te Ara: www.teara.govt.nz.

Local government:
www.teara.govt.nz/en/local-and-regional-government
Entries for Northland, Auckland, Waikato, Bay of Plenty, Taranaki, East Coast, Whanganui, Manawatu, Hawke's Bay, Wairarapa, Wellington, Nelson, Marlborough, West Coast, Canterbury, Otago, Southland, Stewart Island/Rakiura; Chatham Islands, Kermadec Islands, Subantarctic Islands, Antarctica, Pacific Islands and New Zealand

Tourism
Tourism NZ www.tourismnewzealand.com; http://media.newzealand.com/en/story-ideas/new-zealand-regions/

Regional Tourism Organisations New Zealand www.rtonz.org.nz/rto-location-map.html
New Zealand Tourism Guide www.tourism.net.nz

GOVERNMENT

Census 2013 http://www.stats.govt.nz/Census/2013-census/profile-and-summary-reports

Department of Conservation/Te Papa Atawhai www.doc.govt.nz/parks-and-recreation/places-to-go/national-parks/; www.doc.govt.nz/nature/habitats/marine/marine-reserves-a-z

Local Government NZ www.lgnz.co.nz

Local Councils www.localcouncils.govt.nz

Land Information New Zealand/Toitū te whenua www.linz.govt.nz; https://data.linz.govt.nz

New Zealand Geographic Board/Ngā Pou Taunaha o Aotearoa www.linz.govt.nz/regulatory/place-names/about-new-zealand-geographic-board

New Zealand Immigration www.newzealandnow.govt.nz/regions-nz.

Regional Council websites See www.lgnz.co.nz/nzs-local-government/new-zealands-councils/

Statistics New Zealand/Tatauranga Aotearoa *Regional population estimates* http://nzdotstat.stats.govt.nz/wbos/Index.aspx?DataSetCode=TABLECODE7501.

Other sites

Government of Tokelau www.tokelau.org.nz
Antarctica New Zealand www.antarcticanz.govt.nz
DairyNZ www.dairynz.co.nz/publications/dairy-industry/new-zealand-dairy-statistics-2014-15
New Zealand Yesteryears http://yesteryears.co.nz/index.html

Using this book in New Zealand classrooms

Within the framework of The New Zealand Curriculum, *Regions of New Zealand* supports the principles of Cultural Diversity and Community Engagement, and the value of Community and Participation. Of the five key competencies that the Curriculum endorses, this book links to Using Language, Symbols and Texts. It also lends itself to the learning area of Social Sciences and to recognising New Zealand's Official Languages.

ACKNOWLEDGEMENTS

The author and publisher acknowledge the kind assistance of Tourism New Zealand, Local Government New Zealand, Land Information New Zealand, the New Zealand Geographic Board and Statistics New Zealand. Our appreciation for expert advice provided by Ron Crosby, Merata Kawharu, Wendy Shaw and Matthew Wright, and valuable input by editor Ross Calman.

Alessandra Zecchini originated the book concept and oversaw design and photo research as the book reached fruition under the assured guidance of editorial director Carolyn Lagahetau and designer Cheryl Smith, while Belinda Cooke provided marketing direction. Special thanks to Arantxa and Max Zecchini Dowling for their editorial assistance.

PHOTO CREDITS

Admir Mullaaliu: p.27 Nelson view, centre of NZ

Alessandra Zecchini: p.8 Waiheke Island; p.9 Karekare; p.10 Huka Falls; p.17 Pania; p.21 Whanganui River; p.25 Picton; p.29 Gold panning, Hokitika; p.31 Little Regent Street, Tekapo; p.34 Kea

ASB Polyfest/Ben Campbell Photography: p.9 Polyfest

Bence Kovacs: p.17 Gannets

Bigstock: www.bigstockphoto.com p.20 Mt Ruapehu

Christchurch City Council: p.4 Canterbury Provincial Council Building

Krzysztof Pfeiffer: p.25 Waihopai Valley; p.35 Stewart Island

Nelson Tasman Tourism: p.27 Nelson cathedral, Farewell Spit

Peter Dowling: p.17 Wairoa; p.29 Franz Josef Glacier

TAG Oil: p.19 Sidewinder plant

Tourism New Zealand: p.7 Bay of Islands (Alistair Guthrie); p.9 Eden Park and Auckland; p.11 Hobbiton (Ian Brodie), Waitomo Caves (Corin Walker Bain); p.13 Whakaari/White Island (Chris Sisarich), Lake Tarawera (Mark Smith), Woodcarving (James Heremaia); p.14 Eastwoodhill (Tourism Eastland); p.15 Gisborne City (Ray Sheldrake); p.19 New Plymouth (Rob Tucker); p.21 Palmerston North (Destination Manawatu), Manawatu landscape (Destination Manawatu); p.22 Castlepoint (Daniel Rood); p.23 Weta workshop (Weta Workshops); p.25 Queen Charlotte Sound (Rob Suisted); p.26 Abel Tasman National Park (Fraser Clements); p.30 Canterbury Plains (David Wall); p.31 Aoraki/Mount Cook (Paul Lemlin), Kaikoura seals (Matt Winter); p.32 Lake Wanaka (Wanaka Tourism); p.33 University of Otago (David Wall), Yellow-eyed penguin (Penguin Place); p.34 Invercargill (Venture Southland); p.35 Milford Sound (Rob Suisted)

Shutterstock (www.shutterstock.com): p.6 Tane Mahuta; p.7 Meeting house, Cape Reinga; p.11 Hot Water Beach; p.13 Tauranga; p.15 Sponge Bay Island, Paikea; p.16 Napier; p.18 Dawson Falls; p.19 Mount Taranaki; p.20 Mount Ruapehu; p.23 Kapiti Coast, Cable car; p.24 Vineyard; p.29 Punakaiki; p.33 Baldwin Street, Moeraki Boulders; p.35 Southland; p.37 Antarctica

Published by Oratia Books, Oratia Media Ltd, 783 West Coast Road, Oratia, Auckland 0604, New Zealand (www.oratia.co.nz).

Copyright © 2017 Peter Dowling
Copyright © 2017 Oratia Books (published work)
The copyright holders assert their moral rights in the work.

This book is copyright. Except for the purposes of fair reviewing, no part of this publication may be reproduced or transmitted in any form or by any means, whether electronic, digital or mechanical, including photocopying, recording, any digital or computerised format, or any information storage and retrieval system, including by any means via the Internet, without permission in writing from the publisher. Infringers of copyright render themselves liable to prosecution.

ISBN 978-0-947506-35-3

First published 2017
Printed in China